YOUR KNOWLEDGE HAS VALUE

Sandra Miller

A Short Analysis of Rudyard Kipling's "Below the Mill Dam"

GRIN Publishing

Bibliographic information published by the German National Library:

The German National Library lists this publication in the National Bibliography; detailed bibliographic data are available on the Internet at http://dnb.dnb.de .

Imprint:

Copyright © 2004 GRIN Verlag GmbH
Print and binding: Books on Demand GmbH, Norderstedt Germany
ISBN: 978-3-656-91100-5

This book at GRIN:

http://www.grin.com/en/e-book/293526/a-short-analysis-of-rudyard-kipling-s-below-the-mill-dam

GRIN - Your knowledge has value

Since its foundation in 1998, GRIN has specialized in publishing academic texts by students, college teachers and other academics as e-book and printed book. The website www.grin.com is an ideal platform for presenting term papers, final papers, scientific essays, dissertations and specialist books.

Visit us on the internet:

http://www.grin.com/

http://www.facebook.com/grincom

http://www.twitter.com/grin_com

A Short Analysis of Rudyard Kipling's story "Below the Mill Dam"

"Below the Mill Dam" is set at Robert's Mill in the English countryside at or about the time of the story's publication (1902). Rudyard Kipling had just returned from Africa, where he had experienced the disastrous effects of the Boer War and witnessed such things as the British invention of concentration camps. He was alarmed by the ignorance of British politicians: "Conservative Balfour government's dead cultured aristocratic hand barred the way to a wider, less class-ridden British Empire" (Wilson 226). Kipling was pessimistic that Britain could uphold her imperial role as the world's leading nation, moreover, he was "extremely uneasy with, and critical of, unquestioned traditions, ruling-class hierarchies, and complacent establishments" (Lee 12). Fairly late in his life, in 1902, Kipling decided to live in Sussex in England. Shortly after, he had electricity installed in his house – which was not common at that time – and a sign that he was generally interested in and fascinated by new technology; he installed a turbine, a generator and associated equipment in the watermill in his own garden.

Allegorical or symbolic tales, such as "Below the Mill Dam" convey Kipling's passion for machinery and technology. The story reflects Kipling's views about the changing environment, political atmosphere and the technical innovations that were transforming industry and the modes of production in farming, their impact on the landscape and on living conditions. Kipling disguised his plot as a fable, probably to avoid resentment from the establishment. In writing a political fable, he was able to express his "alarm and dismay at England's apparent inability to address herself socially, imperially, culturally and technologically to the future" (Page 69). Kipling uses allegorical language throughout the

1

dialogues as a means of mockery and satire about forces which want to preserve tradition against the new emerging forces that are pressing for change and development.

"Below the Mill Dam" is an allegory, in which Kipling assigned roles to his protagonists in order to depict different social classes. The Grey Cat and the Black Rat, anthropomorphised animals, act as main characters. Together with the animated characters of the Wheel, the Waters and the Millstones, they converse about past and present events and, in doing so, express controversial points of view, according to their designated social positions. Cats and rats are natural enemies in reality, but in Kipling's fable their natural roles have been suspended; they are allied in their mutual concerns, in other words, they accommodate the status-quo of the British upper classes. The characters of the Black Rat and the Grey Cat are defined by their distinctive use of the English language in dialogues. Their particular way of speaking connotes their social standing and condescending attitudes. The Grey Cat's laziness and how she clings on to her entrenched privileges symbolizes the decadence of the English gentry and the traditional elitist class which controls the House of Lords. The Black Rat's complacency is a reflection of the 'Old English Officer class', mainly recruited from British aristocracy.

Their antagonists are the Waters who represent progress and endorse technological innovation as the new driving force. Also, the Waters work as a counterpoint to the old-fashioned, slow, obsolete wheel and put stress on it to work harder. Their strength, as well as confidence, is reflected in the statement "'We lifted that wheel off his bearings,' cried the Waters. 'We said, 'Take away that bauble!'" (Kipling 290). The Waters, combined from various sources and merged into an immense power on their way to the mill, are busy, forward-pushing and bossy characters, constantly demanding more activity from the old Wheel.

Kipling made a point of using Latin, a dead language, in his characterization of the Wheel as a relic of the past. In perpetually remembering, repeating and reliving ancient times, going as far back as to the Chronicles of English History, the Wheel is depicted as a parody of the Domesday Book "And all the time [...] the senile wheel itself is pouring out its rambling anti-ruling class historical liturgy: 'Book, book, book, book. Domesday Book" (Wilson 244). The Wheel, in union with the animal characters, contemplates the good times and the old times; they do not want or even anticipate a change in the status-quo.

The Millstones reject the Wheel's pretentious concerns for their welfare and assure that they can bear their load as long as the Wheel keeps performing and provides them with the necessary energy. They embody the working class, common people who do as they are told. They accuse the Wheel of being hypocritical for its concerns about rare plants, these 'delicate jewels of nature' but having no regrets for killing the carter's son. (Kipling 292) The Wheel states arrogantly its mere function as "the trituration of farinaceous substances", which is an elaborate, old-fashioned and pompous way of referring to 'the grinding of corn' (Kipling 298).

Gradually the Wheel comprehends that it has gone past its use for grinding wheat but is still "slow to realize that it is being used for electricity, not flour" (Lee 19). Eventually, the Wheel ceases its attitude of clinging on to the past as it gradually accepts and embraces the new technology, electricity and turbines, which will enable continuous work and prospect. The Spirit of the Mill has transferred from the old Wheel into the new turbines, and, together with the Waters, they form the driving power of the future, the avant-garde of progress.

The voices of a farmer and his engineer advisor, the only human characters in the narrative, occur only at the end of the story, introducing the flooding of the dark spaces of the mill with electric light, a metaphor which announces the new era. They put an end to the spoilt feline's uselessness, the one who catches 'no mice', by throwing the Cat into the water. Later, the engineer kills the Black Rat, places it in a showcase for preservation and declares it a rare relic of a bygone era, soon to become extinct and to be succeeded by a new breed.

With the use of a parable as a form of narration, Kipling left the conventions of realism and moved into the fable genre, a subtle literary device, which made it possible for him to avoid direct attacks on the real parties concerned, but to be obvious enough to alert his fellow countrymen and countrywomen about "the impermanence of dominion, the inevitable decline and succession of empires" (*Dictionary of Literary Biography*). His perception of world changes urged him to express a warning to the British people about the inevitable fate of Britain losing its position as a leading nation or being destroyed by a superior power, if there was no willingness to accept new conditions and rules in life. The story can also be evaluated and interpreted as a plea for modernity, based on the idea that social transition has its material basis in technology and Kipling's personification, animism and anthropomorphism in storytelling serve to illuminate that point.

Works Cited

Kipling, Rudyard. "Under the Mill Dam." *Traffics and Discoveries*. Ed. Hermione Lee.

Harmondsworth: Penguin Classics, 1987. 287-303.

Lee, Hermione. Introduction to *Traffics and Discoveries*. Harmondsworth: Penguin Classics,

1987. 7-29.

Page, Norman. *A Kipling Companion*. London: Macmillan,   1989.

Naufftus, William F. (ed.). "Rudyard Kipling." *Dictionary of Literary Biography*, Vol. 156

(British Short-Fiction Writers, 1880-1914). Winthroop University, 1996. 181-199.

Wilson, Angus. *The Strange Ride of Rudyard Kipling: His Life and Works*. London: Secker &

Warburg, 1977.